You Have Only
One Problem

You Have Only One Problem

Experience the Instant Reward of Trustful Surrender

CONOR GALLAGHER

TAN Books
Gastonia, North Carolina

You Have Only One Problem: Experience the Instant Reward of Trustful Surrender
© 2023 Conor Gallagher

All rights reserved. With the exception of short excerpts used in critical review, no part of this work may be reproduced, transmitted, or stored in any form whatsoever, without the prior written permission of the publisher. Creation, exploitation and distribution of any unauthorized editions of this work, in any format in existence now or in the future—including but not limited to text, audio, and video—is prohibited without the prior written permission of the publisher.

Scripture quotations are from the Douay-Rheims Bible. Excerpts from the English translation of the *Catechism of the Catholic Church*, Second Edition, © 1994, 1997, 2000 by Libreria Editrice Vaticana–United States Catholic Conference, Washington, D.C. All rights reserved.

Cover & interior design and typesetting by www.davidferrisdesign.com

Library of Congress Control Number: 2022948291
ISBN: 978-1-5051-3047-8
Kindle ISBN: 978-1-5051-3048-5
ePUB ISBN: 978-1-5051-3049-2

Published in the United States by
TAN Books
PO Box 269
Gastonia, NC 28053

www.TANBooks.com

Printed in India

"All that happens to us in this world against our will (whether due to men or to other causes) happens to us only by the will of God.... Show Him respect by accepting it from His hand, believe firmly that He does not send it to us without cause."

—*Saint Augustine of Hippo*

*To all those I have wrongly perceived
as being problems in my life. Thank you
for being a gift from God.*

Dear Reader,

I, your unworthy author, must emphasize two points in my spiritual writings: the first is regarding the writing style, and the second is a vital disclaimer.

Regarding style, I have adopted a rather antiquated style of writing. Spiritual writers of old spoke directly to the reader with phrases like "Christian Reader" or "Immortal Soul" or even "Unworthy Christian." Modern sensitives emphasize the first-person plural pronouns of "we" and "us" in an unnecessary attempt to avoid the appearance of paternalism or arrogance. So, when I address "you," as the reader, I am truly saying "we," for the message of this work is intended for myself as much as anyone.

Additionally, my favorite works of spirituality have a very particular voice. It is a voice that calls the reader to conversion, as if the author has but one page, one paragraph, one single sentence to convert the reader to Jesus Christ. Such a voice is starkly different from an intellectual work intended to convince the reader's mind of a superior argument. Here, I hope to jar your soul to conversion with the power and beauty of truth, for your soul and those within your care will be in heaven or in hell ten trillion years from now. We all need a little jarring.

Now, a vital disclaimer: I beg you, remember that preaching and doing are two different things. In fact, I find that I gravitate towards projects in which I need the most improvement.

Sincerely,

Conor Gallagher

PRAYER OF SURRENDER

Heavenly Father,

I know You are here. I know You can hear me and see me. You know my every thought and emotion, my dreams and fears. You know all of my perceived problems. You know the reason for my little aggravations and my great sufferings. Your infinite love has chosen each of these perceived problems to be a remedy for my sins and a path to my eternal salvation. Forgive me, Lord, for my failure to accept these sufferings from Your loving hand.

Throughout these pages, enlighten my mind and open my heart. Give me the grace to see beyond the perceived problems in my life. Help me see Your fatherly love in every suffering that comes upon me.

Grant me the wisdom and purity of heart to see with celestial clarity that my only real problem is that I have yet to trustfully surrender to Your providence. In Your infinite mercy, use these pages to enkindle in my soul an unquenchable desire to fully surrender to You so that I may not only experience eternal happiness in paradise but also enjoy peace and happiness right now, even amidst the trials and tribulations of this earthly life.

Amen.

CONTENTS

Introduction 1

Chapter 1: The Perceived Problems 6
    Suffering
    People
    Money
    Your God-Given Limitations
    Sickness and Death

Chapter 2: The One Problem 14
    The Infinity of God
    Trustful Surrender
    Why Every Moment Is Perfect
    The Divine Physician

Chapter 3: The Reward 24
    Sanctification
    Peace and Happiness in This Life
    The Happiest Moment in History
    Always Get What You Always Want

Chapter 4: What You Become to Others 32
    Wise Listener
    Wise Counselor
    True Friend

Chapter 5: The Last .1 Percent 40
    The Tin Cup
    What 99.9 Percent Really Means
    The Truth Revealed

Conclusion 49

Endnotes 51

Recommended Reading 55

You are ready to eliminate all your perceived problems by focusing on the one fundamental problem that all saints must face.

INTRODUCTION

What if I told you that you could remove *all* of your problems? What if I told you that you could collapse your numerous challenges into *one* problem and that you could resolve all your problems simply by dealing with this one problem?

Imagine what people would pay for a single pill that solved every medical issue from a hangnail to a brain tumor. Imagine if science could find the source of all energy, harness that energy, and apply it universally for movement and power. While those examples are not realistic at the moment, there is a path to freedom from the countless problems that give you anxiety every day.

This is not lip service, hyperbole, or exaggeration. It is real. And the saints do it every day.

If you are like most people, you have a lengthy list of problems.
- Do childhood wounds still haunt you?
- Does marriage conflict leave you exhausted and angry?
- Does financial hardship leave you worried about the future?
- Do colleagues at work irritate you to no end?
- Do adult children break your heart?
- Do you have a sick loved one with whom you would gladly switch places?
- Do you suffer continual failure due to your own shortcomings, whether it be mental, social, or physical?
- Are you confronting death in the near future?

The list could go on forever.

NO NEED FOR PRIORITIZING
If I asked you to list your many problems, big and small, it might take you all day. No doubt, you would add to the list as the day goes on. As soon as you sit in traffic, your list would grow. As soon as you have too many emails to process, your list would grow. As soon as you have to deal with an insurance company, your list would grow. As soon as you look at your full schedule, your list would grow.

When you try to diagnose your problems, when you try to grapple with them, you become overwhelmed. Often, the best advice you are given is to "prioritize them" and start chipping away at them one at a time.

While this is good advice, it fails to provide the real solution. Why? Well, if you solved your numerous problems tomorrow, aren't you going to have more problems creep back in? Isn't some irritating person, or Mother Nature, or the laws of economics going to return with a vengeance in the near future?

If you reflect on your life you will see that you have "solved" many problems. And yet, they seem to pile up faster than you can off load them.

WHY PROBLEMS PILE ON

There are a few reasons why our perceived problems seem greater than previous generations, despite the comforts and ease of modern resources:

1. **Life Complexity:** Planet earth has reached the greatest levels of complexity. As a result, you are pulled in so many directions due to technology, movement, speed, and secularism. And there seems to be no end to this uncontrollable whirlwind of complexity.

2. **Micro-vision:** In our modern times, we are used to bifurcating everything into as many little pieces as possible. This has trained your brain to see your life (especially the problems) in terms of tiny little pieces, as if your life were an instruction manual with a million pieces.

3. **Sloth:** The devil looks for ways to complicate your life. Complexity breeds sloth. Too much movement breeds sloth. Too much speed breeds sloth.

4. **Pride:** Because you are a member of a fallen race, you sometimes enjoy the drama of problems. The Irish call it the "delicious misery." Part of you, even if only a tiny part, feels important when you have many problems, and perhaps a bigger part of you desires sympathy from others. This is often called the "martyrdom complex."

The modern solutions for addressing these problems will not last. The perfect time management system will not guard you from what you experience as problems. There is no app that will make your problems disappear.

Why?

NO PROBLEMS—PLURAL

Believe it or not, you do *not* have problems—plural. Truly, you have only one problem—one problem that underlines all other perceived problems. You have one problem that springs forth from your soul and infiltrates every aspect of your life.

You are like a bird that flutters about a hundred different branches, never understanding that all the branches make up one tree.

God is watching you, right now, jump back and forth between problems. And He knows all along that there is actually one problem at the core of your soul. And if you could only climb down from all the branches, you could also see the base of this mighty tree that is your life.

"What saint has ever won his crown without first contending for it?"

Saint Jerome

Again, you do not have many problems. You do not have financial problems, or health problems, or social problems, or family problems. Do you have difficulties in these areas? Of course. Do you have tremendous suffering in these areas? Of course. But are they truly problems? In the purest sense of the word, no. These difficulties and sufferings are not necessarily meant to be overcome, conquered, defeated, or solved.

Your one and only one problem is this: you have not completely surrendered your entire being and life to Divine Providence. Once this is done (or at least begun with intent), you will begin to see all the other difficulties and sufferings as from the infinite hand of a loving Father. They are no longer "problems" but gifts—perfectly customized gifts for your salvation.

The good news is that you are not alone in this struggle. Most saints did not become saints overnight. They, too, experienced moments of uncertainty, doubt, anxiety, mental confusion, and intense suffering. Their lives were filled with more "problems" and obstacles than anyone. But with time, they came to see these problems with supernatural faith as their greatest treasures.

CHAPTER 1

THE PERCEIVED PROBLEMS

You no longer need to perceive the sufferings in every area of your life as problems to be solved.

Perception always begins with the senses. You see, hear, smell, feel, or taste. When we speak of a *perceived* problem, let us consider the *mental impression* that results from the sensory input. As a human, you quickly develop a mental impression of what you sense.

Due to the effects of original sin, however, your darkened intellect can easily perceive reality through a selfish, sinful framework. It is as if sin has fogged the lenses through which you see reality: you do not easily see things for what they truly are.

As a result of original sin, human nature "is wounded in the natural powers proper to it; subject to ignorance, suffering, and the dominion of death; and inclined to sin."

Catechism of the Catholic Church 405

As a flawed creature, you must have the humility to realize that your perception may differ from reality. At times, your perception is even skewed, distorted by not only original sin but habitual sin. Years and years of pride, lust, envy, greed, gluttony, anger, and sloth have led you down the wide road to hell rather than up the narrow road to heaven.

SUFFERING

One of the greatest perception problems today is the notion that pain is bad. You have been conditioned by virtually every aspect of your life (especially your natural propensities) to avoid suffering. It is only natural. And it is only natural for those who love you to help you avoid suffering.

From your own experience, however, you know suffering is often the prerequisite to great accomplishment. Whether you train for a marathon, or have a baby, or study for college exams, or work through marital conflict, anything worth doing involves some level of pain.

Think of your heroes. Perhaps they are living. Perhaps they are dead. Which one of them became truly great without suffering? Not a single one. Now, what loving parent would deprive his child of this opportunity? And how is God, dear reader, any different?

> *"Pain and suffering have come into your life, but remember pain, sorrow, suffering are but the kiss of Jesus—a sign that you have come so close to Him that He can kiss you."*
> Saint Teresa of Calcutta

God has never given you a problem. He gives you only exactly what you need at exactly the right moment. Very often, dear Christian, He gives you suffering. Why? Because suffering is something that most often must be endured, experienced, embraced, and converted into something beautiful. Suffering—as difficult as this sounds—is a gift. Mother Teresa once said, "Pain and suffering have come into your life, but remember pain, sorrow, suffering are but the kiss of Jesus—a sign that you have come so close to Him that He can kiss you."

PEOPLE

Most people would admit that other people are their biggest problem—a complaining wife, an angry or lazy husband, an arrogant teenager, an unsympathetic boss, a bull-headed neighbor.

A saint, however, understands that these people are not problems. They may cause much suffering in your life, but they are never problems.

God is infinite. He has the almighty power to customize every moment of your life. This includes every person you ever meet.

Consider this, dear reader: Yesterday you came to a red light beside a stranger in the next lane over. This was not a coincidence. This was not nature unfolding after 13.8 billion years of happenstance. No! It was almighty God's customized plan for you *and* the person in the next lane over. Every encounter with other people is God's perfect plan for you.

> "The Lord maketh poor and maketh rich, he humbleth and he exalteth."
>
> 1 Kings 2:7

> "Good things and evil, life and death, poverty and riches, are from God."
>
> Ecclesiasticus 11:14

MONEY

Financial stress seems to have a ripple effect in a staggeringly disproportionate manner. For this reason, financial stress is one of the greatest perceived problems. How common it is to say, "I have money problems."

Your free will decides when to save and when to spend. God never controls our free will. But the story of Job teaches that "The Lord gave, and the Lord hath taken away" (Job 1:21). Did Job say the Lord gave and the devil hath taken away? No, the Lord hath taken away. This is a hard reality to accept for the modern mind. Sometimes God unexpectedly blesses people with money, and sometimes He takes it away. He can do this through the laws of economics, by natural disasters, or by simply not intervening when you continue down a destructive path.

The Lord, dear reader, is the Divine Financial Planner. He is not limited to amortization tables; He has infinity on His side. And thus, you do not have money problems any more than Job. Job had an extraordinary invitation by the Lord to entrust his suffering to Him. It is no different with you.

"The sixth degree of humility is that a monk be content with the poorest and worst of everything."

SAINT BENEDICT

YOUR GOD-GIVEN LIMITATIONS

If you are the more reflective type, one of the most difficult perceived problems is your own shortcomings. Perhaps you have a learning disability. Perhaps you are socially awkward. Perhaps you are naturally anxious and therefore twitch and fidget in odd ways to cope. Perhaps you are trapped in a wheelchair.

Now, imagine walking into Michelangelo's studio as he is sculpting his famous statue, *David*. You, who know nothing about sculpting, look at his tools lying on the table. You see oddly shaped chisels and hammers. They look nothing like the chisel and hammer in your garage. Michelangelo reaches for his tool, in fact, the oddest-looking tool on the table. You stop him and abruptly say, "You can't use that! That's the dumbest looking tool I've ever seen. You are about to ruin your sculpture!"

This, my friend, is exactly what you do to the Divine Craftsman when you think He made a mistake in giving you a perceived shortcoming. Every part of you is a tool custom designed by the Divine Craftsman. Your limitations are not problems. Rather, they are the tools for the Divine Craftsman to design you into exactly what He wants you to be.

The great Jesuit spiritual master Father Jean Baptiste Saint-Jure wrote, "We ought to be content with what we have been given and desire nothing more. What we have is sufficient because God has judged it so." The reason so many people are miserable is this: They are not content with whom God made them to be. They want to be somebody else. They want to rid themselves of their defects. But according to Saint Paul, "Power is made perfect in infirmity. Gladly therefore will I glory in my infirmities, that the power of Christ may dwell in me" (2 Cor. 12:9). Dear reader, the more you embrace your weaknesses, the more God's strength will shine through you.

SICKNESS AND DEATH

What greater perceived problem is there than the dreaded C word: cancer? What greater perceived problem is there than a sudden death? How could sickness and death not be a problem, especially when they affect your loved ones so greatly? You know someone who has a serious illness. You know someone who has died "before his time." And you see the sorrowful aftermath in those all around.

God, however, has a time and place for everything. If your son suffers from a grave illness, it is because his infinitely loving Father has chosen him to suffer greatly for some special reason. If your daughter dies, it is because her infinitely loving Father wanted the child for Himself.

While these seem to be life's greatest problems, they are not. They are opportunities granted by God for those who are able to focus on the real problem—the one problem that underlies all of your perceived problems—to which we now turn.

"He who accepts death with perfect resignation acquires similar merit to that of a martyr."

Saint Alphonsus Liguori

CHAPTER 2

THE ONE PROBLEM

Your one problem is that you have not **trustfully surrendered** every single aspect of your life to Divine Providence.

When you read the statement on the previous page, you may have rolled your eyes. You may have thought we were dealing with mere semantics. You may have thought the statement was theologically imprecise. You would be right if we lived in the realm of academics. But we do not. We are called to live in the realm of the spiritual life. And it is in the spiritual life that we find not only great saints but the greatest intellects the world has ever known.

The saints understood that the most important question in life is simply this: have you trustfully surrendered everything to Our Lord? *This* is the reason the saints were so often spared anxiety, doubt, and fear. *This* is the reason they suffered so well. *This* is the reason their success never went to their heads. As Rudyard Kipling said of a true man, "If you can meet with Triumph and Disaster / And treat those two imposters just the same."

The saints saw everything, both the good and the bad, as coming from the hands of God. They did not have problems. They pulled back the layers of their perceived problems and saw that deep within was a test administered by Almighty God, a test that challenged them to accept everything in life as a gift from God. And what loving son or daughter would reject such a gift from a loving father?

> *"I will see the hand of God in all that happens to me, attributing nothing to individual people, who are but instruments used by Him in the work of my sanctification."*
>
> Saint Raphaela Mary of the Sacred Heart

But this is a difficult concept to embrace. It takes some getting used to. It takes some humility. It takes practice. Let us begin.

THE INFINITY OF GOD

"Nothing occurs by chance in the whole course of our lives is the unanimous teaching of the Fathers and Doctors of the Church."[1] This, however, is particularly difficult for modern man to accept.

Our culture has maimed itself with materialism. We simply do not comprehend *infinity* like we used to. To grapple with infinity properly, you must bring the greatest powers of your mind to bear. While you know that God has no limits, it may be difficult to accept that God can calculate the ripple effects of every action of every human to ever live. He can run the algorithm on how you will stub your toe twelve years from now. He does not supersede your free will. But He can read the results of your free will and the trillions of possible outcomes of every little decision you make. The Lord can calculate the effect of every flutter of butterflies' wings throughout all of history.

Truly, it is easier for the infinite God to simultaneously calculate the trillions of possible outcomes of every person's action than for FedEx to track a package. His infinity, dear reader, is something that your mind cannot grasp. But you must, in all humility, accept that the events of your life, even those caused by the sin of others, are all accounted for by the divine algorithms. The calculations of your life alone would have zeros wrapping around the galaxy, but to God, the calculation of everything in existence is as simple as 1+1=2.

"If we could see all He sees we would unhesitatingly wish all He wishes. We would beg Him on bended knees for those afflictions we now ask Him to spare us."

Saint Claude de la Colombière

TRUSTFUL SURRENDER

The etymology of *surrender* has French and Latin roots. The word literally means "to give yourself back to whom you are owed." As God is your author, your creator, your source of being, it is only fitting that your end, your purpose, your final calling is to be given freely back to Him. And of all the 117 billion people who have lived on earth, *you* are the only one who has the power to surrender yourself back to Almighty God.

At its core, trustful surrender means seeing everything from God's perspective. *Everything!* We call this "surrender" because you must humbly submit your will, your hopes, your dreams, your situation, your body, your mind, your relationships, your everything to His will. Metaphorically, you wave the white flag. You give up the fight; that is, you stop trying to control your present and your future. And you stop regretting your past. You accept everything, good and bad, as something carefully prepared for you. And we call this form of surrender "trustful" because you

"Amen I say to you, unless you be converted, and become as little children, you shall not enter into the kingdom of heaven."

Matthew 18:3

are like a child that jumps into the arms of his daddy without a care in the world. There is no fear of falling, because daddy's arms are the safest place in the universe. And no harm can fall upon a child in his father's arms.

Saint Claude de la Colombière, the spiritual director of Saint Margaret Mary, posed the obvious question that you may be asking while at the same time answering it. "But should we attribute it to God when we are unjustly persecuted? Yes, He is the only person you can charge with the wrong you suffer. He is not the cause of the sin the person commits by ill-treating you, but He is the cause of the suffering that person inflicts on you while sinning."[2]

WHY EVERY MOMENT IS PERFECT

When you have accepted the seemingly unacceptable, when you have seen that every difficulty is an act of love for your salvation, your experience of a solitary moment is transformed. Every moment in your life—which includes this one, and this one, and this one—is perfect.

Perfect? Even those moments filled with pain? Even those moments filled with sin?

God perfectly designs every moment to give you the best chance of reaching heaven. Would a loving father ever put his child in an occasion of sin? No. A loving father constructs an environment that is conducive to virtuous living. Unfortunately, you often think you know better than God. And so, you choose creation over the Creator, vice over virtue. But a wise father will use everything, even sin itself, to bring his child back to himself. Hence, even a sorrowful moment is an incredible opportunity for salvation and conversion!

Even though God allows you to sin, He gives you the necessary grace to not only avoid it but also repent of it when you fall. Yes, He constructs every situation for your eternal salvation. Your sin is obviously not perfect. But the moment wherein the sin resides is a carefully constructed moment by Christ for your repentance.

Consider Judas. At the Last Supper, God gave Judas the perfect moment to abide with Himself. Christ even washed Judas's dirty feet, praying that His love might win over his heart. But Judas preferred earthly wealth over heavenly wealth. And so Judas sinned against God by going to the temple priests. Standing before them, God gave Judas another chance to change his mind and join Our Lord in the Garden. He failed again. With every single step towards the Garden with the guards in tow, God gave Judas the perfect moment to divert them elsewhere or to stop and say, "I can no longer do this." But he continued on. Moments later, as he approached Our Lord, ready to betray Him with a kiss, God gave Judas the perfect moment to flee or drop to his knees, begging for forgiveness. And just before he committed suicide, God gave him the perfect moment to repent and to spare his own soul from eternal damnation.

Every single moment is perfect.

THE DIVINE PHYSICIAN

One of the main reasons you have so many perceived problems is because you, like all of us, are doubtful that the most difficult moments are actually redemptive.

And yet, consider how trustfully you surrender to your doctor. You would literally pay a surgeon to pick up a sharp instrument and cut into your flesh to remove a cancer. Would you direct him on exactly where to make the incision? Would you direct him

"Trials and tribulations offer us a chance to make reparation for our past faults and sins. On such occasions the Lord comes to us like a physician to heal the wounds left by our sins. Tribulation is the divine medicine."

SAINT AUGUSTINE OF HIPPO

on exactly how large to make the incision? Would you direct him on exactly how deep to cut? No. You trust this worldly man, who merely went to school for a few years, who is ignorant of the human body far more than he is knowledgeable, whose hands might shake, whose mind might wander, whose soul might become vicious, who might even sneeze at the wrong moment. And yet, you throw yourself into his hands, pleading with him to cut with haste, and paying him money to do so.

How silly you must now feel when you consider the Divine Physician with His own scalpel! Are you still prepared to tell the Divine Physician when to cut, where to cut, how to cut? Are you still prepared to tell God that the surgery is complete and that He must back away from the operating table? Are you still prepared to take the blade from His infinitely steady hand and say, "I know what I am doing?"

When you, dear Christian, can see every difficulty in your life as an incision into your soul by the Divine Physician, brought to you for the sole and exclusive purpose of healing you of self-centeredness and pride and a myriad of other imperfections, then you will understand that your one and only problem is whether you trust the Divine Hand that holds the scalpel.

Not one saint was left untouched by some form of suffering or divine surgery. Was not Saint Paul's temporary blindness and constant health issues a sign from God that his strength came from God alone? Was not the cannonball that shattered Saint Ignatius of Loyola's leg a sign from God to convert his wayward soul? Were not the deaths of Saints Louis and Zélie Martin's four children a nudge towards detachment from this passing world?

If you look around the world, you will see that you are not the only one who suffers. No, everyone must suffer. In fact, the

"We can only go to heaven through suffering, but it is not all that suffer who find salvation. It is only those who suffer readily for the love of Jesus Christ, who first suffered for us."

Saint Vincent de Paul

saints suffered as much as any class of people. But they did not suffer for the sake of suffering but rather because God ordained it. They knew that the Divine Physician had a reason for their suffering, whether it was to make atonement for their past sins or for the sins of others. Dear reader, never forget the words of Saint Faustina, who once said, "If the angels were capable of envy, they would envy us for two things: one is the receiving of Holy Communion, and the other is suffering."[3] Next time you suffer, call upon your guardian angel, who looks with the greatest compassion on your pain, and who would gladly trade places with you. Specifically, ask your guardian angel for God's light and grace so that you might suffer with peace and gratitude for being chosen by Christ to help carry His cross.

CHAPTER 3

THE REWARD

Your reward for trustful surrender is not only eternal paradise but **peace and happiness** in this life.

Consider whether you have ever done an act purely out of love for God or, if you are like most of us, you always have some ulterior motive when you perform spiritual and corporal works of mercy. When you pray for the dead, are you not hoping that someday they will pray for you when they reach heaven? When you feed the homeless, are you not hoping that God will remember you when you come into His kingdom?

You do not deserve much blame for this. It was God Himself who infused you with self-preservation. Still, you may consider purifying your motives by increasing your selflessness and decreasing your selfish impulses.

Because God is a loving Father, He offers us not only the eternal reward of Himself but also an earthly reward for surrendering ourselves to Him. And He wants you to experience this immediate reward. He even wants you to seek this immediate reward.

God is not hiding this gift from you. He has no desire to surprise you with peace and happiness. He has told you repeatedly that there is a reward awaiting for you *right now!*

SANCTIFICATION

The obvious reward for trustfully surrendering to Divine Providence is the ultimate reward: paradise. This is obvious, this is simple, but it is not *per se* easy.

As we can see in the life of Christ, what is easy can also turn your heart to stone. It is easy to believe that your salvation is found in the routine practice of traditions, like the scribes and Pharisees. Christ showed little patience with those who ruthlessly held the letter of the law over the heads of the vulnerable.

> *"Woe to you scribes and Pharisees, hypocrites; because you are like to whited sepulchers, which outwardly appear to men beautiful, but within are full of dead men's bones, and of all filthiness."*
>
> Matthew 23:27

Clinging to the law can become the antithesis of trustful surrender. It can become a heretical notion that in order to be saved, you must do rituals in this or that precise way, as if God is bound by words and subtle motions. Such clinging to the practices and procedures of our Faith can be a prideful way of believing that God is indebted to us rather than the opposite. In other words, "I did these things just right, and so You must give me heaven."

When you place your faith in externals, you enter the realm of many, many problems. You feel the pressure to perform each and every religious gesture with a ritualistic purity. You feel a need to outperform your fellow Christians. You feel the need to rattle off more and more prayers. Yes, you must pray, for there is no hope of heaven without sincere prayer and repentance. But without trustfully surrendering to God's will, your prayers are nothing but lip service to Him. And like the scribes and Pharisees, you can easily become "whited sepulchers" (Matt. 23:27).

PEACE AND HAPPINESS IN THIS LIFE

The less obvious rewards for trustful surrender in this life are peace and happiness. This can be seen on both a natural and supernatural level.

On a natural level, you experience peace when numerous problems are removed. Think of the last time you made an extensive to-do list and the sight of it was overwhelming. The list was like a tsunami of anxiety and fatigue. But imagine if someone took away the list and said, "I will handle everything on this list except for your first priority. Go and focus on that one thing. Leave the rest to me." Imagine! You would feel not only relief from the many smaller problems but also energized to go tackle your number one priority.

On a supernatural level, God desires that you be at peace *right now*! As the Divine Physician, He may well send you suffering for the purpose of spiritual healing. But suffering and peace are not mutually exclusive.

Trustful surrender causes all of your perceived problems to dissipate instantly, for you believe that God ordains everything for your salvation. When you solve your one true problem, the grace of Almighty God washes away the many perceived problems that previously debilitated you. You are then free to experience the peace and happiness that has always awaited you.

THE HAPPIEST MOMENT IN HISTORY

Consider the good thief on the cross, Saint Dismas. He hung in agony, struggling to take every breath. There was no chance of survival. No friends or family would take him from the cross. He would either hang for days or have his legs broken to expedite the suffocation. But what did he do, Christian reader? In his last moments, he surrendered to Jesus Christ, asking for mercy. "Lord, remember me when thou shalt come into thy kingdom" (Luke 23:42). And as the face of Jesus turned towards him, stained with blood from the crown of thorns, Dismas felt a moment of anticipation. How would Our Lord respond? In what seemed like an eternity in Dismas's mind, Our Lord gave the greatest pardon ever, "Amen I say to thee, this day thou shalt be with me in paradise" (Luke 23:43). He did not say *you'll eventually be with Me.* He did not say *you'll be with My angels in paradise.* He said that *this day,* Dismas, you will be with *Me* in paradise. Imagine the peace and happiness that overshadowed the agony of the cross! In fact, Dismas could have asked Our Lord to miraculously spare his bodily life, but he did not. Do you think Dismas, the good thief who stole heaven, would have traded paradise in order to come down from the cross? I don't think so. And nothing in Dismas's life could ever compare to the peace and happiness that he felt at that moment while hanging in agony on a cross.

But Saint Dismas's peace came only after the greatest war of his life, the war for his soul. Unlike Judas, Dismas repented because he realized that all of his problems boiled down to one problem: whether or not his heart and his will were surrendered to the Man dying next to him. Certainly, the devil was tempting Dismas to despair, but grace was calling Dismas to trust. In his moments of intense agony, Saint Dismas experienced a light from the cross. He realized that the Romans were no longer his problem, his wounds and sins from his life were no longer his problem, his inability to physically bow before Jesus was no longer his problem. Paradise was now in Saint Dismas's soul because he discovered the secret of peace and happiness in this life: surrender.

Some mystics attribute Saint Dismas's conversion to Our Lady's prayers at the foot of the cross. After all, she was the most perfect woman of surrender and the queen of martyrs. Her entire life involved preparing her Son for His passion and death. And if our Lady can help Dismas in his final moments, what can she do for you right now?

Dear Christian reader, the happiest moments of Saint Dismas's life were experienced while he was dying on a cross. Where are your peace and happiness to be found?

ALWAYS GET WHAT YOU ALWAYS WANT

It may sound trite. It may sound contrived. It may sound like a Christian gimmick. But the lives of the saints prove otherwise. You can always get what you always want. If you only desire the will of God, then everything that happens to you is exactly what you want to happen to you.

You experience this phenomenon in minute ways with those you love. Have you ever had a sick child and wanted to do what they *wanted you to do?* You love them so much that you just wanted to be of service. It was not an inconvenience for you to suffer a little for them. You *wanted* to do something to show your love. In a way, the greater the sacrifice you could make for them, the better it would make you feel. What loving parent would not *gladly* take the cancer away from their child? Would he do this begrudgingly? No! He would do it because he wants to.

When you love God above yourself, you desire to experience what He has prepared for you. It is as if the Divine Author has written your story out of love, and you desperately desire to see how everything plays out.

There is no gimmick. If you truly love the Lord, you want only what He wants.

The perfect prayer, dear Christian reader is this: *Lord, I wish to only wish what you wish,* or best spoken by Our Lord Himself, *Fiat Voluntas Tua* ("Thy will be done") (Matt. 6:10).

"Neither dost thou fear God, seeing thou art condemned under the same condemnation? And we indeed justly, for we receive the due reward of our deeds; but this man hath done no evil. And he said to Jesus: Lord, remember me when thou shalt come into thy kingdom."

LUKE 23:40–42

CHAPTER

4

WHAT YOU BECOME TO OTHERS

You become a completely unique and awe-inspiring force in people's lives without even trying.

Friendship is a beautiful thing. It is sad, however, how many friendships perpetuate the experience of numerous perceived problems.

You know the situation. You go seeking sympathy from a friend. That friend gives you what you think you want. They help you try to resolve the practical issue before you. They do their best. They agree with you that the "problem" is awful. And their compassion, their love, their friendship zeros in on how to resolve the "problem."

> *"I have called you friends: because all things whatsoever I have heard of my Father, I have made known to you."*
>
> John 15:15

There is nothing wrong with this *per se*. There is nothing wrong with resolving issues in our lives. But often what is lacking is another layer of true Christian friendship. A saintly friend finds a creative and gentle way to not only ease the suffering of the sufferer but also encourage him to embrace the event as a gift from God. True Christian friendship spurs on the other to the highest form of virtuous living. He is not preachy. He is not harsh. He is not unsympathetic. He is not aggressive in evangelizing his hurting friend. Above all, he asserts with patience and kindness that surrender is the key to unlocking the peace and happiness amidst the pain and sorrow.

Imagine that friend in your life. Imagine that voice in your ear. Imagine that arm around you. Imagine that shoulder to cry on. How much closer can you get to Christ?

WISE LISTENER

When you have trained yourself to see perceived problems as a fully customized, personal gift from the hand of God, you tap into a wisdom rarely found in this life.

As a friend or stranger talks to you and explains his plight, you listen with a new pair of ears. You not only hear him, but you listen with an attention like never before. You listen to the facts, you listen to the emotions, you listen to the complexity of the situation. But because you are also listening for the voice of God in the situation, you listen beyond his words. It is as if the motives of the other people in the story become perfectly transparent. You see the movement of their hearts and the longing of their souls. It is as if God has given you the gift of listening with angelic simplicity, for the earthly complexity melts away after you have trustfully surrendered.

WISE COUNSELOR

At Confirmation, the Holy Spirit gave you a tremendous power to advise your relatives and friends in times of trouble. It is the gift of counsel. It is a staggering tragedy that more of us do not invoke this gift that rests within our soul, awaiting to bloom at a moment's notice.

When you are surrendered to the will of God, your advice takes on a completely different character. First, you are likely to give different comfort or advice precisely because you see the situation in a unique way. Second, even if you say virtually the same thing as another person, you are likely to say it with such simplicity and clarity that the plain meaning of your words sink deeper into the other's soul.

"Love everyone with a deep love based on charity . . . but form friendships only with those who can share virtuous things with you. The higher the virtues you share and exchange with others, the more perfect your friendship will be."

SAINT FRANCIS DE SALES

Most importantly, however, you will find kind and creative ways to explain what his perceived problems center on. And you will be able to do this without criticism, without belittling his suffering, without trivializing his grief. Perhaps most importantly, you will not just help him solve this or that particular issue. Rather, you will show him how to deal with every single issue that will ever arise. It is the supernatural version of teaching a man to fish rather than giving him one to eat.

TRUE FRIEND

Since the dawn of time, man has been trying to figure out that special, unique, and compelling relationship that we call *friendship*. You can easily imagine our most ancient ancestors living in caves, working together to fight off predators, carrying the injured on one's shoulders, or playing tricks on each other. Since this time, man has wrapped his arm around another when his child died. He has advised him not to be reckless. He has metaphorically and literally talked him off the ledge.

Aristotle believed friendship was one of the most important human dynamics to understand. You can have, he contends, three forms of friendship. First, you have pleasure friendships. Consider buddy relationships, which are mostly present in childhood. These are people you have fun with but perhaps not much more than that. Second, you have utility friendships. Consider moms or dads who are "friends" with other couples so the kids can get together, or work colleagues, or even your local barber. Once the usefulness ends, the relationship dissipates. Lastly and most

> *"A faithful friend is a strong defence: and he that hath found him, hath found a treasure."*
>
> Ecclesiasticus 6:14

importantly, you have virtuous or "true" friendship. Here you have both people striving for virtues but also helping the other person strive for virtue. This mutual assistance in virtue is staggeringly powerful.

If you have ever had a true friendship, you are very blessed. Most of us will go a lifetime without a single one.

But if you are trustfully surrendered to Our Lord, you will quickly become a true friend to others. You will not reside long in pleasure friendships or utility friendships. You will know that God placed this friend in your life for a particular reason.

When you are certain that God has placed a person in your path, you are far more likely to tap into the most important aspects of life rather than residing in mere pleasure or utility. And your gift to this person is so contagious that your friend is likely to reciprocate and become the same true friend to you. Yet again, we see trustful surrender being its own reward.

"God sends us friends to be our firm support in the whirlpool of struggle. In the company of friends we will find strength to attain our sublime ideal."

SAINT MAXIMILIAN KOLBE

CHAPTER 5

THE LAST
.1 PERCENT

You are ready and able to take an extraordinary shortcut to **total surrender** by figuring out the very last thing you would surrender, passionately offloading this final perceived problem.

Throughout this little book, you have seen many types of perceived problems. You have seen what the one problem truly is. And you have seen the incredible reward that awaits you. And still, you tell yourself, "This is easier said than done."

While this is partially true, there is a significant shortcut offered to you by your infinitely merciful Father. He wants you to struggle in certain ways, for that is the path of growing in love. But He categorically, emphatically does not want you to have a long path to surrender. He is willing to do anything to help you surrender right now. And thus, He offers you a shortcut—for lack of a better word.

Imagine you are a saint. In other words, imagine you are someone who has fully embraced the liturgical life, the sacramental life, and the spiritual life that tradition has to offer. You live for others. You pray out of love rather than duty. Your confessions are filled with mostly sins of omission rather than commission. And you are greatly detached from this world.

But there is one thing that you still struggle with. There is one thing that still returns to haunt you on a regular basis. You ask God if He will ever spare you of this struggle. It is the last thing your heart is attached to. You have given, let us imagine, 99.9 percent of yourself to God! But there is this last .1 percent remaining. It is still yours.

The question for you, dear Christian reader, is *what is that last .1 percent*? And if you can name it, you can surrender it.

THE TIN CUP

There is a story of a very holy man who had given his life to Our Lord. Whereas once he slothfully struggled to even attend Mass, he learned to pray without ceasing and with zeal. And grace

> *"He who possesses God lacks nothing: God alone suffices."*
> Saint Teresa of Ávila

helped him overcome the sins of the flesh. He no longer lusted after women. He saw, in fact, every woman as an image of Our Lady. He no longer indulged in gluttony with food and drink. He became, in fact, so detached from his stomach that he had to be reminded to eat to keep up his strength. He no longer snarled at others in anger when he was offended and no longer arrogantly looked down at the specks in the eyes of others. He was, people would say, a walking saint.

Other than the rags that covered his frail body, his only possession was a small tin cup from which he would drink the rainwater he collected or the soup for which he would beg. He carried this tin cup for decades. It was bent and beaten on every side. It was the most pathetic of tin cups to ever remain in the hand of man. But more importantly than the water and soup, the tin cup held many memories for the old man. It had traveled with him on pilgrimage. When he looked in the cup, he could see the faces of the poor he served with it throughout the years. It represented to him the many trials and tribulations of his journey to God. It was his prized possession. It was his only possession.

One solemn day, the old saint for the millionth time offered himself entirely to God. He heard a voice. "Will you give me everything?" "Yes, Lord, of course. I have already given you

"In the evening of this life, I shall appear before You with empty hands, for I do not ask You, Lord, to count my works. All our justice is stained in Your eyes. I wish, then, to be clothed in Your own Justice and to receive from Your Love the eternal possession of Yourself. I want no other Throne, no other Crown but You, my Beloved!"

SAINT THÉRÈSE OF LISIEUX

everything. What else can I give you?" "Give me your tin cup," said the voice of God. At hearing this, a sadness shot through the old man. It was all he had left. Why must he give even that up? Were the many years of service not enough? Was his mind, his body, his heart not enough? Did the Lord really demand a measly tin cup?

The old man wrestled with this request all through the night. He felt heaven slipping away. He felt the Lord withdrawing. It terrified him. He realized that he had given 99.9 percent of himself to his Lord, but not everything. The next morning, he gave the tin cup to the first beggar he could find. The beggar looked with contempt on the gift, for he preferred money or food. It was a great insult to the old man. And it was then he realized that he had now given everything. He was finally free from all the problems in the world. He was filled with grace because he was as empty as the tin cup. He had given up, once and for all, his final problem. He was 100 percent surrendered.

Dear Christian, what is your tin cup?

WHAT 99.9 PERCENT REALLY MEANS

You must consider a difficult truth. Giving 99.9 percent of yourself to God means you have not been willing to give God everything. It means that on some level—even if very unconsciously—you believe that God does not deserve everything, or at least that you deserve to keep something.

This is a hard truth to accept, especially since you are trying to live a holy life. You are a saint in the making. The mere fact that you are reading this book proves that you desire to surrender to your heavenly Father. On the one hand, surrender is not an all-or-nothing proposition. It is not always black or white. Our lives are filled with many gray areas. But on the other hand, the surest way to find peace and happiness is to surrender everything.

At the very least, dear reader, you should recognize that you have not given everything to God, even though God deserves everything. Humility expects that much.

THE TRUTH REVEALED

When you use your imagination and ask the Holy Spirit to help you discover the .1 percent that you are holding back from God, a truth about yourself is revealed. You will begin to see what thoughts, feelings, relationships, possessions, and reputations impede your trustful surrender. Even Abraham was asked to give up his .1 percent—namely, his son Isaac.

A constant exploration of your interior life should include the search for attachments. Where your sin lies, there lie your greatest attachments. You should seek to uncover the chains that are preventing your spirit from soaring to the heavens. You should seek to find the tiny little ideals that reside deep down where you worship them in secret. You should seek to rid yourself of every problem by finding out the last perceived problem you have not yet fully surrendered.

God does not expect you to chip away at every problem one at a time. No! He permits you to cut the tree of self-reliance at the taproot. You need not trim away at every branch. Each of us has a taproot that is buried so deep within our souls that we can barely see a way to detach from it.

Therefore, with all your spiritual and physical energy, with the intercession of your guardian angel and your patron saint, offer this deeply rooted attachment to Our Lord immediately. Once you do so, you will find that the branches of your many other attachments come tumbling down with ease.

> "Hold back nothing of yourselves for yourselves so that He who gives Himself totally to you may receive you totally."

SAINT FRANCIS OF ASSISI

You are ready to trustfully surrender, not 80 percent, not 90 percent, not 99.9 percent of yourself to Divine Providence, but **100 percent.**

CONCLUSION

A great marathon runner was asked how he ran a marathon in just over two hours. He answered by asking how in the world someone could run a marathon for four hours!

The truth of the matter, dear Christian reader, is that the hardest thing in the world to do is to give yourself partially to God and partially to the world. With such an arrangement, you are a person without a home. You are a nomad. And you will never become a saint. As Saint Thérèse of Lisieux once wrote to a young priest, Abbe Maurice Belliere, a few months before her death, "You cannot be half a saint; you must be a whole saint or no saint at all."

You have read in this little book about why you do not have many problems, but only one. You see now that suffering is not the same as a problem to be solved but a gift to be cherished.

> *"You cannot be half a saint; you must be a whole saint or no saint at all."*
>
> Saint Thérèse of Lisieux

Hopefully, you are convinced more than ever that God is infinite, that He is infinitely loving, and that He is *your* infinitely loving Father. Such a father would never allow anything to happen to you, except through your own sinful free will, that was not beneficial to your salvation. Saint Claude de la Colombière reminds you of the Father's infinite love with these stirring words: "Excite in yourself a firm trust that God will provide for all you need, will direct, and protect you with more than a father's love and vigilance, and guide you in such a way that, whatever happens, if you submit to Him everything will turn out for your happiness and advantage, even the things that may seem quite the opposite."[4]

And thus, your only problem is that you have not perfectly surrendered yourself and every aspect of your life to Divine Providence.

When you have done this, peace and happiness are instantly bestowed upon you by your Father, like a king that enthrones his princely son. You may not receive riches, but instead poverty. You may not enjoy health and fitness, but instead weakness. You may not be popular or famous, but instead live in humble obscurity. And your happiness will be found in "even the things that may seem quite opposite."

Remember, dear Christian, that you have only one problem.

Trustfully surrender now and the reward is yours.

ENDNOTES

1. Jean Baptiste Saint-Jure and Claude de la Colombière, *Trustful Surrender to Divine Providence: The Secret of Peace and Happiness* (Charlotte, NC: TAN Books, 1980), 6.

2. Saint-Jure, 86.

3. Saint Maria Faustina Kowalska, *Divine Mercy in My Soul: Diary of Saint Maria Faustina Kowalska* (Marian Press, 2003), no. 1804.

4. Saint-Jure, *Trustful Surrender*, 86.

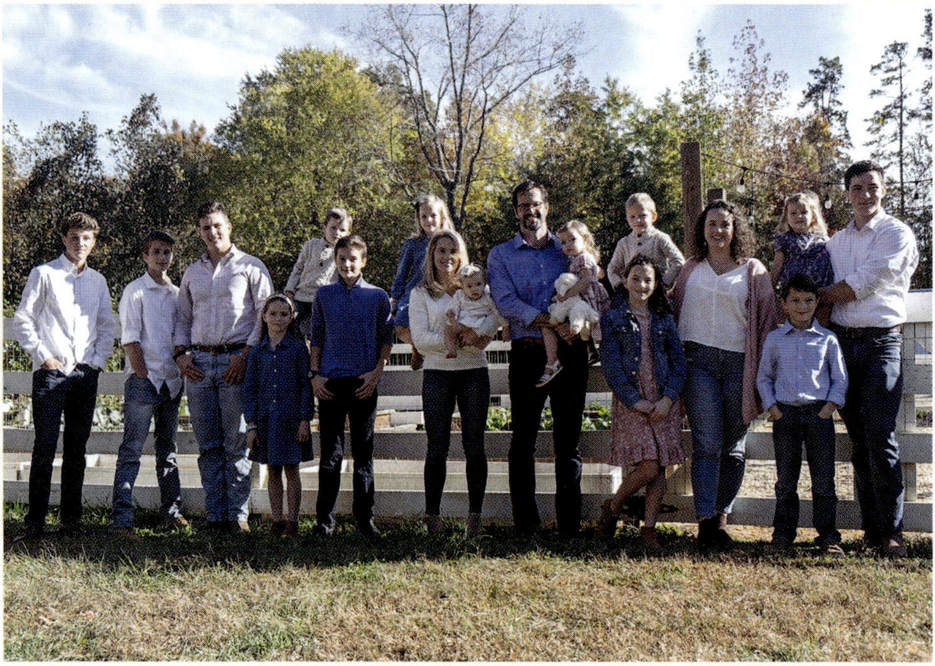

THE AUTHOR

Mr. Conor Gallagher earned both his masters in philosophy and juris doctorate from the Catholic University of America. He began his professional career as a law clerk to the Honorable Robert J. Conrad, chief judge of the Western District of North Carolina. He has been an adjunct professor of philosophy, political philosophy, and Catholic social doctrine at Belmont Abbey College.

Mr. Gallagher has served on many boards, including the Board of Visitors for the Columbus School of Law at the Catholic University of America, the Association of Catholic Publishers, and more recently, the Board of Trustees for Holy Angels, a residence for more than eighty disabled individuals. Currently, Mr. Gallagher serves on the Board of Advisors at Saint Joseph College Seminary, the minor seminary for the Diocese of Charlotte, and the Board of Trustees at Belmont Abbey College. He is also the founder and executive director of the Benedict Leadership Institute at Belmont Abbey College.

Mr. Gallagher is currently the CEO of Good Will Publishers and its subsidiary, TAN Books. He is a regular speaker at parishes, homeschool conferences, and Legatus chapters, and he is often a guest on numerous radio programs, podcasts, and TV shows. He is the author of *Parenting for Eternity: A Guide to Raising Children in Holy Mother Church* (TAN Books, 2021), *Still Amidst the Storm* (TAN Books, 2018), and *If Aristotle's Kid Had an iPod* (Saint Benedict Press, 2013). Books to be released in the near future include numerous other books in the TAN Direction series you are holding now, plus a meditative book on the life of Christ titled *The Meekness and Humility of Jesus Christ* and a novel titled *A Stranger Among Us*. He and his wife, Ashley, are the parents of fifteen children and live on a small hobby farm outside of Charlotte, North Carolina.

IMAGE CREDITS

Cover image: Eucharist © Mariusz Szczygiel, Shutterstock.com

p. VIII Suffering Christ, 1660-70 / Murillo, Bartolome Esteban (1618-82) / Spanish / Caylus Anticuario, Madrid, Spain / Photo credit: Bridgeman Images

p. 4 St. Jerome praying before a rocky grotto, 1548 (oil on panel) / Hemessen, Jan Sanders van (c.1504-66) / Dutch / Photo credit: Johnny Van Haeften Ltd., London / Bridgeman Images

p. 11 St. Benedict, 1487 (oil on canvas) / Memling, Hans (c.1433-94) / Netherlandish / Museo Pinacoteca San Francesco, San Marino / Photo credit: Bridgeman Images

p. 13 St. Alphonsus Liguori / Date: 1913 / Italian / Source: https://en.wikisource.org/wiki/Page:Catholic_Encyclopedia,_volume_1.djvu/375 / Licensing: Public domain, via Wikimedia Commons

p. 18 Claude de la Colombière / Source: http://santiebeati.it/immagini/?mode=view&album=41150&pic=41150.JPG&dispsize=Original&start=0 / Licensing: Public domain, via Wikimedia Commons

p. 21 Portrait of Saint Augustine of Hippo receiving the Most Sacred Heart of Jesus, by Philippe de Champaigne, 17th century / Source: Los Angeles County Museum of Art: https://collections.lacma.org/node/171584 / Licensing: Public domain, via Wikimedia Commons

p. 23 Portrait of Saint Vincent de Paul / François, Simon (1576-1660) / French / Musee et Domaine National de Versailles et de Trianon, Versailles, France / Photo credit: © Photo Josse / Bridgeman Images

p. 31 A Fragment: The Good Thief (Saint Dismas) / Artist: Perino del Vaga (1501–1547) / Source: Royal Collection: https://www.royalcollection.org.uk/collection/402869/a-fragment-the-good-thief-saint-dismas / Licensing: Public domain, via Wikimedia Commons

p. 36 Saint Francis de Sales, 18th century (painting) / Pianca, Giuseppe Antonio (1703-57) / Italian / Palazzo Bianco, Genoa, Italy / Photo credit: Luisa Ricciarini / Bridgeman Images

p. 39 Maximilian Kolbe (colour litho) / Photo credit: Fototeca Gilardi / Bridgeman Images

p. 44 Portrait of Saint Therese of the Child Jesus (or Lisieux or Sainte-Face, 1873-1897) / Photo credit: © Patrice Cartier. All rights reserved 2022 / Bridgeman Images

p. 47 St. Francis of Assisi Receiving the Stigmata (oil on canvas) / Guercino (Giovanni Francesco Barbieri) (1591-1666) / Italian / Museo Pinacoteca San Francesco, San Marino / Photo credit: © NPL - DeA Picture Library / Bridgeman Images

p. 62 Saint Francis of Sales praying behind an altar. Etching by A. Voet / Source: https://wellcomecollection.org/works/zaag6ntb / Licensing: (CC BY 4.0) https://creativecommons.org/licenses/by/4.0/deed.en, via Wikimedia Commons

p. 64 Father St. Pius of Pietrelcina (Francesco Forgione called Padre Pio da Pietralcina, 1887-1968), 1960s (b/w photo) / Photo credit: Fototeca Gilardi / Bridgeman Images

p. 68 The Apostle Paul / Artist: Rembrandt (1606–1669) / Source: National Gallery of Art, Washington D.C. / Licensing: Public domain, via Wikimedia Commons

p. 73 Portrait of Saint Teresa of Calcutta © DeepGreen, Shutterstock.com

RECOMMENDED READING

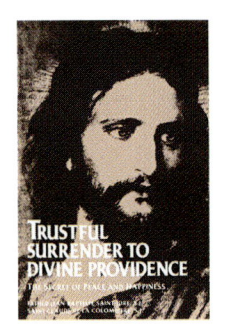

Trustful Surrender to Divine Providence: The Secret of Peace and Happiness

To trust in God's will is the "secret of happiness and content," the one sure-fire way to attain serenity in this world and salvation in the next. *Trustful Surrender* simply and clearly answers questions that many Christians have regarding God's will, the existence of evil, and the practice of trustful surrender, such as:

- How can God will or allow evil?
- Why does God allow bad things to happen to innocent people?
- Why does God appear not to answer our prayers?
- What is trustful surrender to Divine Providence?

This enriching classic will lay to rest many doubts and fears, and open the door to peace and acceptance of God's will. TAN's pocket-sized edition helps you to carry it wherever you go, to constantly remind yourself that God is guarding you, and He does not send you any joy too great to bear or any trial too difficult to overcome.

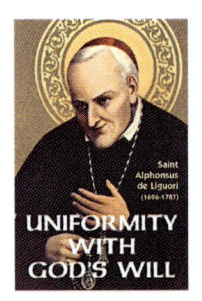

Uniformity with God's Will

In this timeless thirty-two-page booklet, Saint Alphonsus de Liguori spells out what it takes to become a saint. In his own words, *"A single act of uniformity with the divine will suffices to make a saint."* The way to perfection is simple—unite your will with God's and put into action the prayer *"Thy will be done."*

Whether you are struggling with prayer, suffering from an illness, or being persecuted by others, this booklet is a constant reminder that conforming our wills to God's will is the secret to sanctity. Above all, doing God's will is the only way to reach heaven.

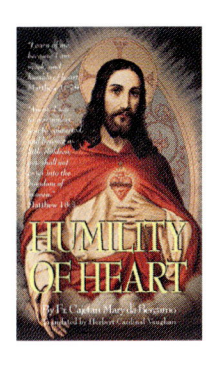

Humility of Heart

Surrendering our perceived problems to Our Lord is simply not possible without the virtue of humility. Indeed, true humility naturally leads to surrender.

This is the greatest book on humility ever written and will likely be the best book you will read in the next five years (outside of Holy Scripture).

Here is how the book opens up:

"In Paradise there are many Saints who never gave alms on earth: their poverty justified them. There are many Saints who never mortified their bodies by fasting or wearing hair shirts: their bodily infirmities excused them. There are many Saints too who were not virgins: their vocation was otherwise. But in Paradise there is no Saint who was not humble."

Below are a few more gems of wisdom contained in *Humility of Heart*. Fr. Cajetan da Bergamo has assembled in this incomparable Catholic classic every conceivable motive for us to practice the virtue of humility.

- "It is only by the measure of thy humility that thou canst hope to please God and save thyself, because it is certain that God 'will save the humble of spirit'" (Ps. 33:19—page 60).
- "As Paradise is only for the humble, therefore in Paradise everyone will have more or less glory according to his degree of humility" (page 75).
- "Humility generates confidence, and God never refuses His grace to those who come to Him with humility and trust" (page 93).

From every direction, he marshals up the reasons why this virtue is paramount in the lives of all saints and of all those on the way of perfection. As no one will enter heaven who is not perfect and as no one will gain perfection who is not humble, it behooves us all to apprise ourselves of the requisites for gaining true humility of heart, for once possessing this virtue, we can then make great strides in the spiritual life. But without it, we are simply deceiving ourselves regarding our spiritual progress and postponing the great work of our own salvation.

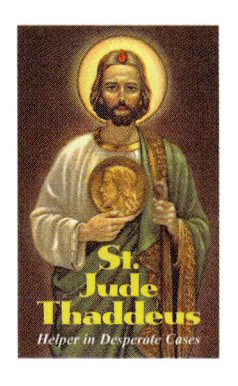

St. Jude Thaddeus

This little booklet is filled with stories and miracles concerning this great saint along with prayers and novenas. In desperate circumstances, the faithful have always turned to Saint Jude Thaddeus—apostle, cousin of Our Lord, and martyr for the Catholic faith. This powerful Saint is invoked in cases of extreme need, grievous illness, poverty, and when circumstances seem hopeless.

Saint Jude is also a special defender of (and helper in regaining) purity. Saint Jude has obtained remedies and comfort for countless people who have turned to him in prayer. In all of our problems, let us seek Saint Jude's intercession.

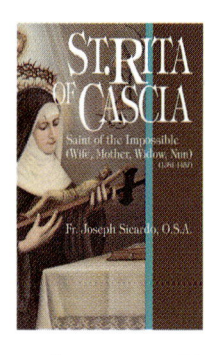

St. Rita of Cascia: Saint of the Impossible

This short, but powerful biography details the life of Saint Rita, who is known as the "Saint of the Impossible."

Desirous of being a nun, Saint Rita instead obeyed her parents and married. Her husband was cruel and caused her much suffering, to which she responded with love and prayers and eventually converted him. After the death of her husband and two sons, Rita was able to enter a convent, where she devoted herself to prayer and penance.

She abandoned herself totally to God, diminishing herself as He increased in her. An inspiring story of a soul completely resigned to God's will.

RECOMMENDED READING

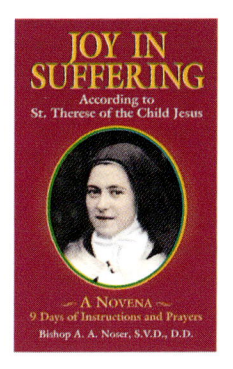

Joy in Suffering: According to St. Therese of the Child Jesus

In this little book, a novena of instruction and prayers, Bishop Noser sets forth Saint Therese's "secrets" for dealing with sufferings of body, heart, and soul. Even though a person may feel bad, and even though a person is still plagued by faults and failings, Saint Therese reveals how to live each moment such that one's life is immensely fruitful for eternity, and nothing will be wasted.

Joy in Suffering shows how the Catholic faith possesses the key to solid peace and joy, even in the most painful situations of life. This beautiful book will help you transform your sufferings into joy!

Abandonment to Divine Providence: How to Fulfill Your Daily Duties with God-Given Purpose

"Let go and let God." This popular phrase captures the essence of Father Jean-Pierre de Caussade's eighteenth-century treatise on trust, *Abandonment to Divine Providence.*

Do you doubt? Do you suffer? Are you anxious about the trials of life?

Father de Caussade offers the one sure solution to any spiritual difficulty: abandon yourself entirely to God by embracing the duties of your station in life. With wisdom and gentleness he teaches how to practice complete submission to the will of God in every situation, whether we are beginners or seasoned travelers on the way of perfection. True abandonment, he explains, is a trusting, peaceful, and childlike surrender to the guidance of grace.

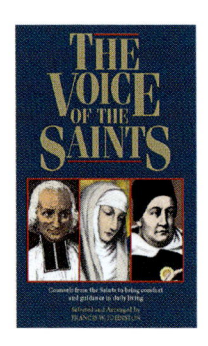

The Voice of the Saints: Counsels from the Saints to Bring Comfort and Guidance in Daily Living
Outside of Our Lord's words, the greatest wisdom shared to mankind are the words of the saints. In this book, you will find over 700 quotes from the saints arranged by various topics like: humility, the power of prayer, the meaning of suffering, and temptation.

As "out of the abundance of the heart the mouth speaks" (Matt. 12:34), so the saints are able to distill an encyclopedia of meaning into just a few words. In this book, we can reap the benefit of their spiritual counsel. All of life's difficulties have a solution: surrendering to God and following the saints' examples.

RECOMMENDED PRAYERS

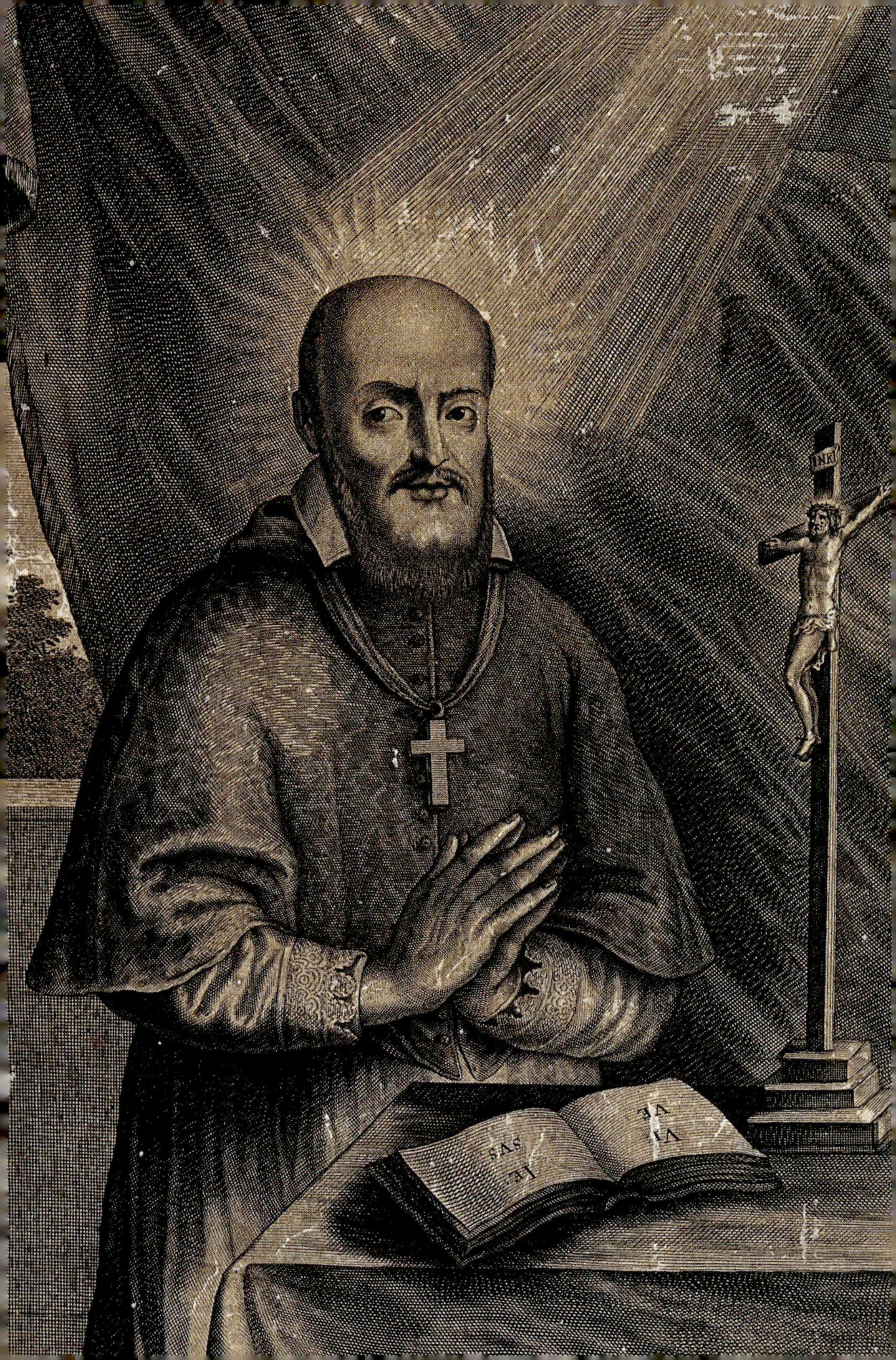
INRI

ACT OF ABANDONMENT
By Saint Francis de Sales

O my God, I thank you and I praise
you for accomplishing your holy
and all-lovable will without any regard for mine.
With my whole heart,
in spite of my heart,
do I receive this cross I feared so much!

It is the cross of Your choice,
the cross of Your love.
I venerate it;
nor for anything in the world
would I wish that it had not come,
since You willed it.

I keep it with gratitude and with joy,
as I do everything that comes from Your hand;
and I shall strive to carry it without letting it drag,
with all the respect
and all the affection which Your works deserve.

Amen.

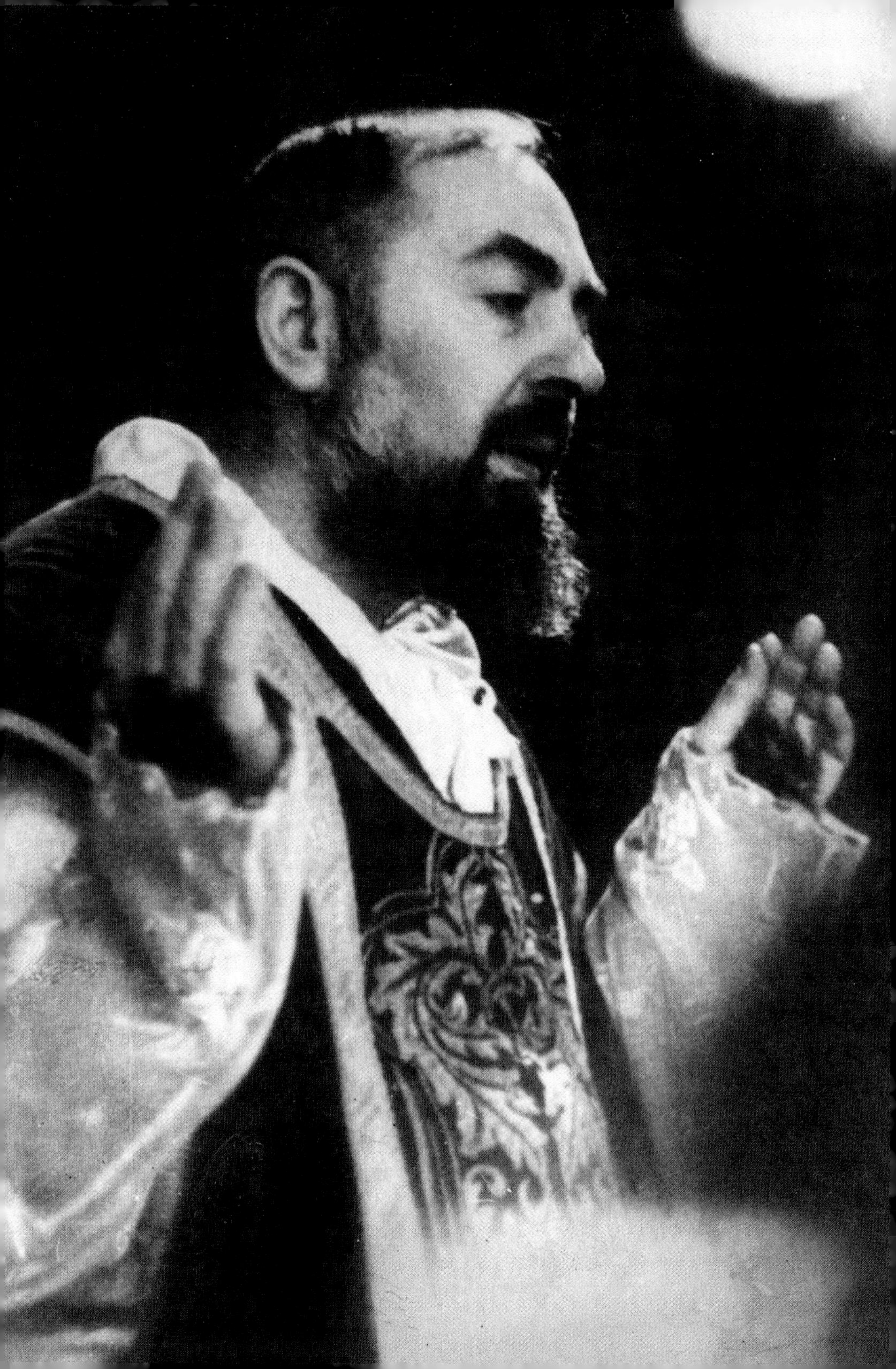

PRAYER OF TRUST AND CONFIDENCE

By Saint Padre Pio

O Lord, we ask for a boundless confidence and trust in Your divine mercy, and the courage to accept the crosses and sufferings which bring immense goodness to our souls and that of Your Church.

Help us to love You with a pure and contrite heart, and to humble ourselves beneath Your cross, as we climb the mountain of holiness, carrying our cross that leads to heavenly glory.

May we receive You with great faith and love in Holy Communion, and allow You to act in us, as You desire, for Your greater glory.

O Jesus, most adorable heart and eternal fountain of Divine Love, may our prayer find favor before the Divine Majesty of Your Heavenly Father. Amen.

AN EXERPT FROM ANOTHER
BOOK IN THIS SERIES...

You Are Never Too Busy

Seeing Your Time the Way God Sees It

CONOR GALLAGHER

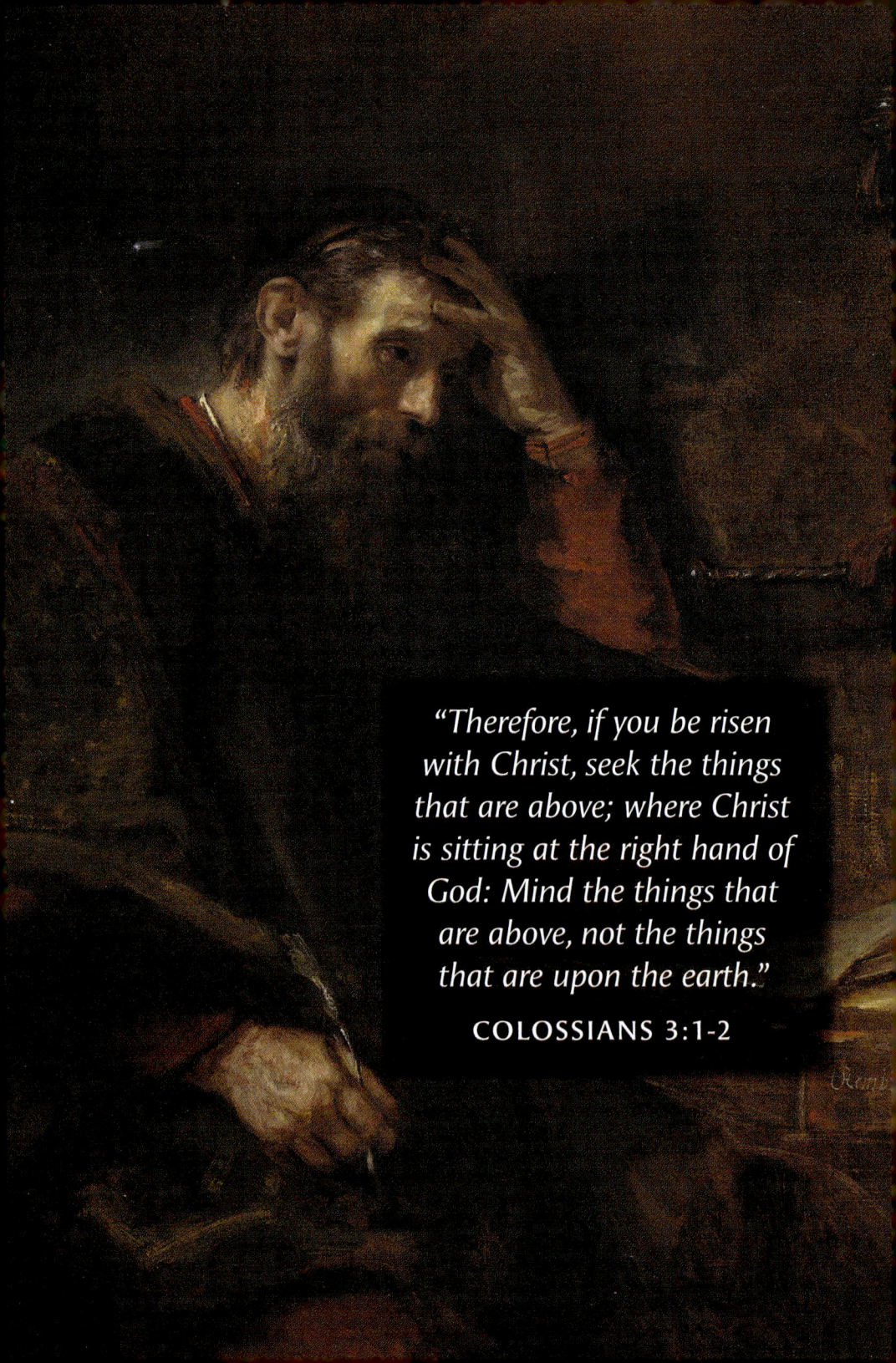

"Therefore, if you be risen with Christ, seek the things that are above; where Christ is sitting at the right hand of God: Mind the things that are above, not the things that are upon the earth."

COLOSSIANS 3:1-2

CONTENTS

Introduction — 1
   "My Yoke Is Sweet"
   Bragging about Being Busy Is a Thing of the Past
   Imagine the Person You Will Become
   Never Too Busy Again

Chapter 1: What Does Busy Mean? — 6
   First Definition: Occupied
   Second Definition: Bustling
   Third Definition: Meddling
   Fourth Definition: Full of Distracting Details

Chapter 2: Your Secret Sin — 16
   The Myth of Productivity
   The Sin of Sloth
   The Devil's Trojan Horse

Chapter 3: All the Time You Need — 26
   Never Waste Your Duties
   Others Cannot Make You Too Busy
   Stress Is Gone
   Freedom in the Minutes
   Plenty of Time for Unconditional Surrender

Chapter 4: God's Two Ways of Freeing You from Busyness — 36
   The First Way God Frees You: Stop Doing Something
   The Second Way: Fail

Conclusion — 45

Recommended Reading — 51

The Lord will

free you from

busyness

INTRODUCTION

Have you wondered how the saints were able to accomplish so much with so little time? How Saint John Vianney was able to hear confessions for hours and still find time for his own prayer life? How Pope Saint John Paul II could visit so many countries, write so many encyclicals, and still shepherd the entire Church?

And how about Saint Teresa of Calcutta? Bring your imagination to bear. Picture Mother Teresa, a seventy-year-old religious sister with a hunched back and aching knees, serving the sick and poor in the scorching heat of India. She answers letters until 11:00 p.m., only to rise at 4:30 a.m. the following morning. She attends Mass and makes a Eucharistic holy hour before beginning manual labor by 8:00 a.m., feeding and bathing grown adults who are too sick to do it themselves. She herself eats virtually nothing. Above all, she performs these tasks with a smile on her face—a smile that she chooses out of love, even if she doesn't feel like it.

Throughout her day, Saint Teresa of Calcutta is constantly interrupted. While changing a grown man's diaper, her religious sister asks her whether they should pay the electric bill or buy food. A repair man then asks whether she wants to just patch the roof or replace the entire section. Then a doctor informs her that the small child in her facility needs a leg amputation because the gangrene has gone above the knee. As the bookkeeper whispers that they can't pay for both the roof and the amputation, an AIDs victim vomits on her. And she must at once bathe and change into another sari while the bookkeeper, the repair man, and the doctor are all waiting on her.

This goes on, dear Christian reader, from before sunup to after sundown. And this occurs decade after decade. You might see this sequence as chaotic. But it was not. It was perfect. Mother Teresa was not busy. She was, at each moment, trying to do the will of God. Franticness might have been felt by the bookkeeper, by the repair man, or by the doctor, but not by Mother. She was not busy.

And neither must you be busy.

"MY YOKE IS SWEET"

"Come to me, all you that labour, and are burdened, and I will refresh you. Take up my yoke upon you, and learn of me, because I am meek, and humble of heart: and you shall find rest to your souls. For my yoke is sweet and my burden light" (Matt. 11:28–30).

Herein lies the secret to never being busy again: you always have the perfect amount of time to do the will of God. Nothing else matters. "Too many things to do" no longer matters. Failure, in fact, no longer matters. Fully appreciating this insight gives you tremendous peace, no matter the chaos in your life.

> *"I do not pray for success, I ask for faithfulness."*
>
> Saint Teresa of Calcutta

At this moment, God wants to bestow one of His greatest gifts on you. He wants to give you the freedom to live like a saint—that is, to do exactly what you are supposed to do in the exact amount of time He gives you to do it. This freedom comes without anxiety or stress because you now have all the time you need to fulfill your duties. Remind yourself of this constantly. You will begin to feel God's peace in only a few moments.

BRAGGING ABOUT BEING BUSY IS A THING OF THE PAST

Being busy might not be what you think it is. It really means that you are, in a manner of speaking, lost or out of control. It means the world has more power over you than God does. It means others have enslaved you. It might mean that you aren't minding your own business. You might not want to tell everyone from here on just how "busy" you are. It is not a point worth bragging about. It is, in fact, the opposite. We will see why shortly.

With God's grace, you are about to see precisely why you should never be busy again. This does not mean you will never have a lengthy to-do list. This does not mean you will never have to move fast or overcome logistical obstacles with family and friends.

But it does mean that you will never think you are too busy to do what really matters. It means that the things that don't get done will be as much of a blessing (maybe more so) as the things you do get done. It means that you will learn how to "meet triumph and disaster, and treat these two imposters just the same," as Rudyard Kipling says in his poem "If." Your failures, dear Christian soul, may well be God's will. And thus, you will never be too busy to do God's will. Or as Saint Teresa of Calcutta would often say, "I do not pray for success, I ask for faithfulness."

IMAGINE THE PERSON YOU WILL BECOME

Christian soul, imagine the kind of friend you will be, the kind of spouse, the kind of parent, the kind of stranger others will meet on the street. Look around. Many people's faces, body language, and tone of voice reflect their busyness. Frankly, the sin of pride makes every person feel busy—or better yet, important. Most of us believe our time is spent wisely. Humble reflection, however, shows otherwise.

> "Be who God meant you to be and you will set the world on fire."
>
> Saint Catherine of Siena

When you learn that you are not too busy, you encounter each circumstance in a different way than most people. You will consider whether this particular moment is in accordance with God's will. So long as it is, you will be perfectly attentive and present. But when the moment is no longer so, you will graciously depart with little or no concern about what other people think about your departure. It is one of the most freeing experiences in life.

Equally as important, you will become a radically different person to those with whom God wants you to associate. Your attention will be almost superhuman because you are not distracted with other "busy stuff" in your life. You will not feel torn because your mind and body will not be in different places. You will be fully present. You will be a better friend, spouse, and parent immediately.

You are about to begin your journey to total freedom of time. Your time belongs to you and God, no one else. His gift to you is to never be busy again.

NEVER TOO BUSY AGAIN

God desires to remove your stress immediately. Why? Because His yoke is sweet, and His burden is light. You may have to run around town and check off a hundred items on your to-do list, but always with His peace in your heart. Yes, God wants to give you His peace every step of the way.

You will never be too busy to be happy. You will never be too busy to succeed or fail for God. You will never be too busy to surrender to Divine Providence. You will never be too busy to be who God is calling you to be and to do what He is asking of you.

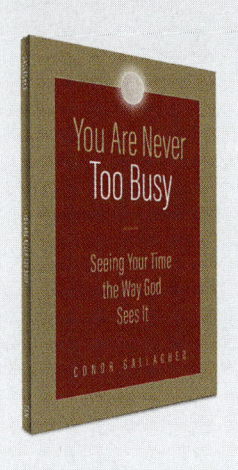

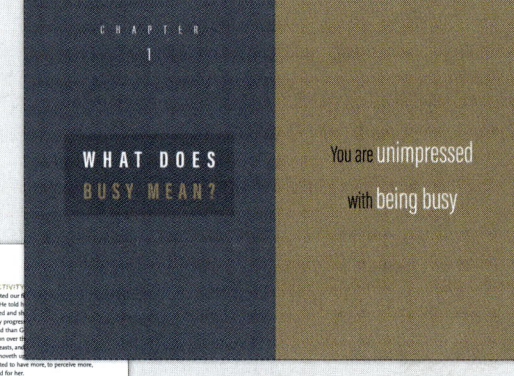

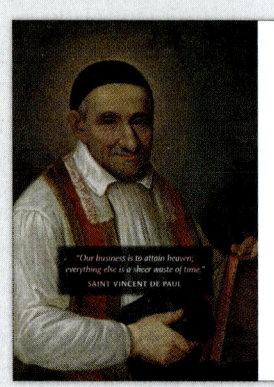

To continue reading, please visit our website at TANBooks.com